START-UP
CITIZENSHIP

THE LOCAL POLICE

Louise and Richard Spilsbury

Evans

Published by Evans Brothers Limited
2A Portman Mansions
Chiltern Street
London W1U 6NR

© Evans Brothers Limited 2007

Produced for Evans Brothers Limited by
White-Thomson Publishing Ltd.
Bridgewater Business Centre, 210 High Street,
Lewes, East Sussex BN7 2NH

Printed in China by WKT Co. Ltd.

Editor: Clare Collinson
Consultant: Roy Honeybone, Consultant in Citizenship
Education and Editor of *Teaching Citizenship*, the
journal of the Association for Citizenship Teaching
Designer: Leishman Design

British Library Cataloguing in Publication Data
Spilsbury, Louise
    The local police - (Start-up Citizenship)
    1. Police - Great Britain - Juvenile literature
    2. Community policing - Juvenile literature
    3. Citizenship - Juvenile literature
    I. Title II. Spilsbury, Richard, 1963-
363.2'3'0941

ISBN-13: 978 0 237 53265 9

Acknowledgements:
Special thanks to the following for their help and
involvement in the preparation of this book: staff, pupils
and parents at Matchborough First School, Redditch,
Mount Carmel RC First School, Redditch and St
Stephen's CE First School, Redditch; David McIlwrick,
Schools Liaison Officer, Southampton Police.

Picture Acknowledgements:
Alamy pp. 4b (Ian Miles-Flashpoint Pictures),
5 (Photofusion Picture Library), 6l (Jack Sullivan), 6r
(Jack Sullivan), 7r (Patrick Eden), 16b (The Photolibrary
Wales); Martyn Chillmaid pp. 11, 12, 13, 14, 16l, 20, 21;
Corbis p. 18l (Herb Schmitz); Getty Images pp. 4t
(The Image Bank/Peter Dazeley), 18cl (Stone/Baerbel
Schmidt); The Guide Association p. 10; iStockphoto.com
pp. 7l, 18cr, 18r; Learning Through Landscapes p. 9;
Southampton Police pp. 8, cover and 15t, title page
and 15b.

Artwork:
Hattie Spilsbury pp. 17, 19.

Contents

Who are the police?

Police are people who help us and other people in our local **community**. How are these police **officers** helping people?

community   officers

Do you wear a school uniform? Police officers usually wear a white shirt, a black jumper or jacket and a black helmet or hat. Why do you think police officers wear uniforms?

Being a police officer is an important job. Why do you think people choose to be police officers?

"I became a police officer because I wanted to be useful to people and to do lots of different things."

uniform   helmet   important

Learning about the police

The police do many different jobs. Police officers patrol the streets to keep people safe. They help people who have been in accidents. They investigate crimes.

▲ These officers are talking to a driver who was going too fast.

▲ This policeman is controlling crowds at a parade. Why do you think police officers wear reflective jackets?

▼ **Police officers have different vehicles. If the police have to get somewhere very quickly, the noisy sirens and flashing lights on their cars warn people to get out of the way.**

▶ **In busy cities some officers ride bicycles because they can get around more easily that way.**

vehicles   sirens

Keeping ourselves safe

A police officer comes to Sam's school to talk about the risks for walkers and cyclists on the roads. They discuss ways of keeping safe.

◀ The officer explains why people should wear helmets when cycling.

He says that it is important to wear something reflective if you are walking or cycling in dim light. Reflective clothing helps drivers to see you.

risks   discuss   role-play

The children take part in a role-play. They pretend to be drivers and pedestrians on a road. Where is it safe to cross the road? What should you do before crossing?

The Highway Code is a set of rules for people who use the roads. These rules keep us safe. What rules would you put in a road safety code?

pedestrians   Highway Code   rules

Rules

Different communities may have different rules. To join a new group you sometimes have to promise to follow their rules.

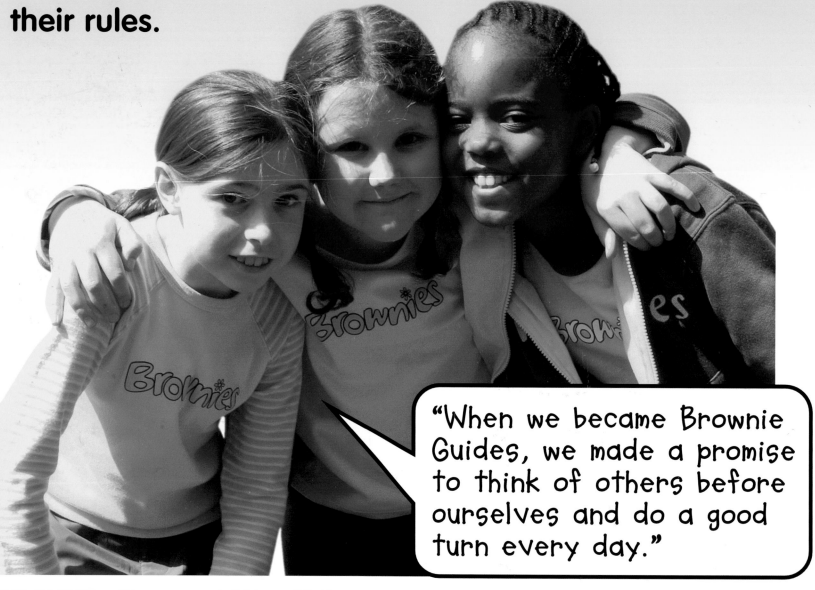

"When we became Brownie Guides, we made a promise to think of others before ourselves and do a good turn every day."

group   promise

Who makes rules? At home parents make the rules. They may make rules about bedtime and what TV programmes you watch. How do rules like this help us?

▲ The children on this school council are deciding on some school rules. The members put their hands up to vote on what rules to include.

How do rules make things fair?

keeping property safe

▶ The children in this class are talking about ways to keep their property safe. They decide to label their things and keep them on their peg or in their tray.

How do you keep your property safe?

Keeping Things Safe

. Put labels on clothes

property

Then the children discuss stealing. Stealing is against the law. Laws are rules made by the leaders of a country that everyone must obey.

◀ Tom uses a doll to say how sad he would feel if someone stole something from him.

What happens to people who break a law?

stealing   law   obey

Visiting a police station

Laura's class plans a trip to the nearby police station. The children read some books about the police and think up questions to ask when they get to the station.

"I want to ask who looks after the police dogs."

Then they look at a local map to find out where the police station is.

police station   questions

► At the police station, an officer explains that some people have to pay a fine if they commit a crime. Others may have to go to prison. Why do we need punishments?

◄ The police dog handler tells the children that his dog lives at home with him. The dog helps him search for missing people and look for stolen property.

fine   commit   punishments   15

Thinking about vandalism

Have you seen pictures of vandalism in a newspaper? Vandalism is when someone damages property for no reason. Vandalism is a crime.

► Vandalism often destroys things that people need. When a park is damaged like this, children cannot use it anymore.

vandalism   damages   destroys

The children in Zac's class invite people from their community to talk about vandalism in the area. People from the local council talk about the costs of repairing damaged property.

MAKE THIS A NICER PLACE TO LIVE!

STOP VANDALISM

▲ The children make a poster to help stop vandalism. What else would you put on a poster like this?

Who else helps us?

There are many people who help us in the community.

parent carer teacher grandparent

friend cook doctor fire officer

▲ Can you match the people in these pictures with their titles? How do people in the community help us in different ways? What would happen if these people were not there?

match   titles

Jasmine's class made a map of their local area. They marked on it the places where people who help us work.

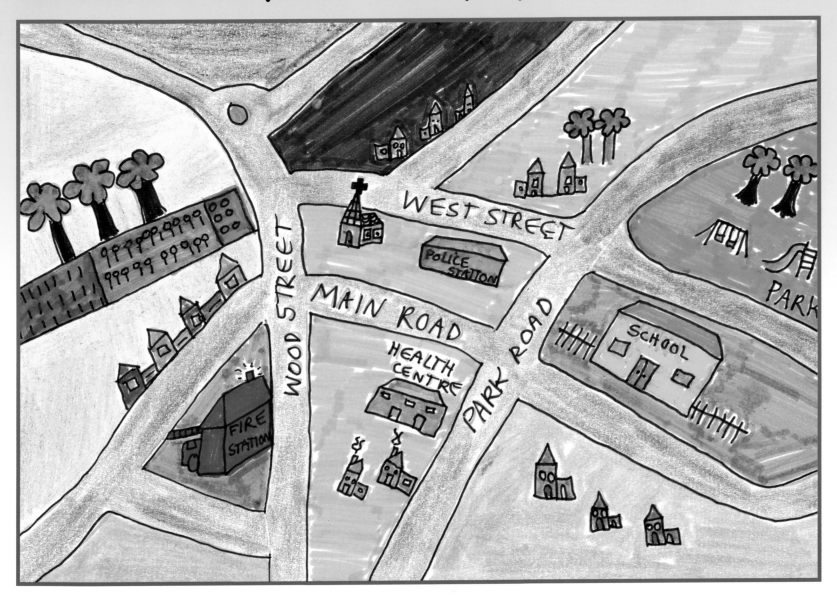

▲ Which street is the fire station in? What is next to the police station? Who works in the health centre?

fire station   health centre

Emergency!

Fire officers and coastguards work for emergency services. What are the other emergency services? What should we do in an emergency?

▲ At school we learn what to do in case of fire. In a fire drill, why do we leave our belongings behind and meet outside?

20   coastguards   emergency   fire drill

Who should we call for help? In an emergency, it is okay to shout or interrupt people. Try to get help from someone you know. Or ask someone who wears a uniform or works in a shop.

◀ If there is no one to help you, dial 999. This is the number for the emergency services. It is free to call. Try to speak clearly and calmly. Say what the problem is and where you are.

interrupt   clearly   calmly

Further information for

New words listed in the text:

calmly	destroys	helmet	obey	punishments	sirens
clearly	discuss	Highway Code	officers	questions	stealing
coastguards	emergency	important	parade	reflective	titles
commit	fine	interrupt	patrol	repairing	uniform
community	fire drill	invite	pedestrians	risks	vandalism
council	fire station	law	police station	role-play	vehicles
crimes	group	match	promise	rules	vote
damages	health centre	members	property	school council	

Possible Activities

PAGES 4-5

You could download a picture of a police officer and ask the children to label parts of the officer's uniform. Discuss the purpose of each part. The children could do the same for police vehicles, too. Or they could draw a police officer and label the different parts of the uniform.

PAGES 6-7

The children could look at Victorian police equipment (a whistle or rattle to raise the alarm and a truncheon) and think how these differ from the modern equipment. At http://www.icons.org.uk/theicons/collection/the-bobby/features/changing-uniform children can read about and see pictures of police uniforms in the past. The children could also investigate how crime and punishment have changed over the course of history. Was it fair years ago? Is it fair now?

PAGES 8-9

At http://www.juniorcitizen.org.uk/kids/roadsafety there are activities to teach children how to be safe in various situations. This includes a spot-the-difference picture in which they have to spot the differences between two cyclists, one wearing the correct gear and the other not.

PAGES 10-11

This is a chance for children to think about their school rules and perhaps talk about others they would add. To help them understand how a school council works they could agree a set of class rules in small groups. One member of each group could be chosen to represent their group and to present their ideas to the class.

PAGES 12-13

To encourage the children to think about why people steal you could give them a scenario as an example, such as someone whose mother was ill at home with no money and everyone in the house was very, very hungry. Ask the children if having an excuse makes stealing okay, or whether it is still wrong.

22

Parents and Teachers

PAGES 14-15

When they get back from a visit to a police station, each of the children could make a poster to show three important things that happen in police stations.

PAGES 16-17

Children could consider the costs of repairing vandalised property and why people vandalise things. They could compile a set of newspaper headlines about vandalism that they collect over a period of time. You could discuss the charity Crimestoppers with the children. An adult can call 0800 555 111 if they want to report a crime such as vandalism, but are unsure about getting involved with the police.

PAGES 18-19

Children could make a classroom display showing people in their community who help them, including teachers and other school staff. Beneath each person they could say how each person helps them. They could think about why some wear uniforms and others do not. Children could match pictures of vehicles and equipment with the people who use them.

Children could prepare questions on a computer to ask a visiting member of the community who helps them. They could sort the questions into different subjects, such as questions about their uniform and questions about what their job involves.

PAGES 20-21

In a drama session you could give one group of children a set of scenarios to act out. For example, the actors could pretend to be lost in a shopping centre, sick or injured, stuck with school work or upset about an argument with friends. Then another group of children could guess what is happening in each scene and suggest what they would do and who they would ask for help. At http://www.firekills.gov.uk/kids/01.htm if you click on Frances the Firefly and then the phone icon, you can go through a script for phoning the Fire Rescue Service. The children could also try to think of other alarms, such as clock alarms, burglar alarms and ambulance sirens. What are these for and why do different alarms have different sounds? They could have some fun making different alarm sounds, perhaps using some musical instruments.

Further Information

BOOKS FOR CHILDREN

History from Photographs: People Who Help Us by Kathleen Cox (Hodder Wayland, 2006)

People Who Help Us: Police Officer by Rebecca Hunter (Cherrytree Books, 2005)

The Police (People Who Help Us series) by Clare Oliver (Franklin Watts Ltd, 2002)

A Day in the Life of a Police Officer by Carol Watson (Franklin Watts Ltd, 2001)

WEBSITES

http://www.askcedric.org.uk/resources

http://www.crimestoppers-uk.org

http://www.devon-cornwall.police.uk/v3/homepage/id-game.html

http://www.homeoffice.gov.uk

http://www.nccl.org.uk/learning_and_access/index.asp

http://www.northyorkshire.police.uk/youth/default.asp

http://www.police.uk

http://www.rospa.org.uk

Index